MznLnx

Missing Links Exam Preps

Exam Prep for

College Algebra

Stewart, Redlin, Watson, 4th Edition

The MznLnx Exam Prep is your link from the texbook and lecture to your exams.
The MznLnx Exam Preps are unauthorized and comprehensive reviews of your textbooks.

All material provided by MznLnx and Rico Publications (c) 2010
Textbook publishers and textbook authors do not particpate in or contribute to these reviews.

MznLnx

Rico
Publications

Exam Prep for College Algebra
4th Edition
Stewart, Redlin, Watson

Publisher: Raymond Houge
Assistant Editor: Michael Rouger
Text and Cover Designer: Lisa Buckner
Marketing Manager: Sara Swagger
Project Manager, Editorial Production: Jerry Emerson
Art Director: Vernon Lowerui

Product Manager: Dave Mason
Editorial Assitant: Rachel Guzmanji
Pedagogy: Debra Long
Cover Image: Jim Reed/Getty Images
Text and Cover Printer: City Printing, Inc.
Compositor: Media Mix, Inc.

(c) 2010 Rico Publications
ALL RIGHTS RESERVED. No part of this work covered by the copyright may be reproduced or used in any form or by an means--graphic, electronic, or mechanical, including photocopying, recording, taping, Web distribution, information storage, and retrieval systems, or in any other manner--without the written permission of the publisher.

Printed in the United States
ISBN:

For more information about our products, contact us at:
Dave.Mason@RicoPublications.com

For permission to use material from this text or product, submit a request online to:
Dave.Mason@RicoPublications.com

Contents

CHAPTER 1
Prerequisites — 1
CHAPTER 2
Equations and Inequalities — 12
CHAPTER 3
Coordinates and Graphs — 22
CHAPTER 4
Functions — 26
CHAPTER 5
Polynomial and Rational Functions — 33
CHAPTER 6
Exponential and Logarithmic Functions — 39
CHAPTER 7
Systems of Equations and Inequalities — 41
CHAPTER 8
Matrices and Determinants — 44
CHAPTER 9
Conic Sections — 53
CHAPTER 10
Sequences and Series — 57
CHAPTER 11
Counting and Probability — 62
ANSWER KEY — 65

TO THE STUDENT

COMPREHENSIVE

The *MznLnx* Exam Prep series is designed to help you pass your exams. Editors at MznLnx review your textbooks and then prepare these practice exams to help you master the textbook material. Unlike study guides, workbooks, and practice tests provided by the texbook publisher and textbook authors, *MznLnx* gives you **all** of the material in each chapter in exam form, not just samples, so you can be sure to nail your exam.

MECHANICAL

The MznLnx Exam Prep series creates exams that will help you learn the subject matter as well as test you on your understanding. Each question is designed to help you master the concept. Just working through the exams, you gain an understanding of the subject--its a simple mechanical process that produces success.

INTEGRATED STUDY GUIDE AND REVIEW

MznLnx is not just a set of exams designed to test you, its also a comprehensive review of the subject content. Each exam question is also a review of the concept, making sure that you will get the answer correct without having to go to other sources of material. You learn as you go! Its the easiest way to pass an exam.

HUMOR

Studying can be tedious and dry. MznLnx's instructional design includes moderate humor within the exam questions on occassion, to break the tedium and revitalize the brain

Chapter 1. Prerequisites 1

1. The _____ are natural numbers including 0 ' href='/wiki/0_(number)'>0, 1, 2, 3, ...) and their negatives (0, −1, −2, −3, ...). They are numbers that can be written without a fractional or decimal component, and fall within the set {...

   a. AKS primality test
   b. Integers
   c. ADE classification
   d. Abelian P-root group

2. In mathematics, a _____ is any number that can be expressed in the form

$$\frac{a}{b}, a, b \in \mathbb{Z}, b \neq 0$$

which says 'a divided by b, given that a and b are integers and b does not equal zero'. Since the denominator b may be equal to 1, every integer is a _____. The set of all rational numbers is denoted $\mathbb{Q}$ (for quotient.)

   a. Number system
   b. -equivalence
   c. Rational number
   d. Ratio

3. _____ is the mathematical process of putting things together. The plus sign '+' means that numbers are added together. For example, in the picture on the right, there are 3 + 2 apples--meaning three apples and two other apples--which is the same as five apples, since 3 + 2 = 5.

   a. ADE classification
   b. Abelian P-root group
   c. AKS primality test
   d. Addition

4. In mathematics the _____ of a set which is equipped with the operation of addition is an element which, when added to any element x in the set, yields x. One of the most familiar additive identities is the number 0 from elementary mathematics, but additive identities occur in other mathematical structures where addition is defined, such as in groups and rings.

   - The _____ familiar from elementary mathematics is zero, denoted 0. For example,

     5 + 0 = 5 = 0 + 5.

   - In the natural numbers N and all of its supersets (the integers Z, the rational numbers Q, the real numbers R, or the complex numbers C), the _____ is 0. Thus for any one of these numbers n,

$$n + 0 = n = 0 + n.$$

Let N be a set which is closed under the operation of addition, denoted +. An _____ for N is any element e such that for any element n in N,

$$e + n = n = n + e.$$

   a. Identity element
   b. External
   c. Universal algebra
   d. Additive identity

5.   In mathematics, especially in elementary arithmetic, _____ is an arithmetic operation which is the inverse of multiplication.

Specifically, if c times b equals a, written:

$$c \times b = a$$

where b is not zero, then a divided by b equals c, written:

$$\frac{a}{b} = c$$

For instance,

$$\frac{6}{3} = 2$$

since

$$2 \times 3 = 6.$$

In the above expression, a is called the dividend, b the divisor and c the quotient.

   a. -module
   b. 2-bridge knot
   c. -equivalence
   d. Division

Chapter 1. Prerequisites 3

6. In algebraic geometry, divisors are a generalization of codimension one subvarieties of algebraic varieties; two different generalizations are in common use, Cartier divisors and Weil divisors The concepts agree on non-singular varieties over algebraically closed fields.

A Weil _____ is a locally finite linear combination (with integral coefficients) of irreducible subvarieties of codimension one.

   a. Picard group
   b. Lefschetz pencil
   c. Divisor
   d. Linear system of divisors

7. In mathematics, the complex numbers are an extension of the real numbers obtained by adjoining an imaginary unit, denoted i, which satisfies:

$$i^2 = -1.$$

Every _____ can be written in the form a + bi, where a and b are real numbers called the real part and the imaginary part of the _____, respectively.

Complex numbers are a field, and thus have addition, subtraction, multiplication, and division operations. These operations extend the corresponding operations on real numbers, although with a number of additional elegant and useful properties, e.g., negative real numbers can be obtained by squaring complex (imaginary) numbers.

   a. Complex number
   b. -equivalence
   c. -module
   d. 2-bridge knot

8. In mathematics, and more specifically set theory, the _____ is the unique set having no (zero) members. Some axiomatic set theories assure that the _____ exists by including an axiom of _____; in other theories, its existence can be deduced. Many possible properties of sets are trivially true for the _____.
   a. ADE classification
   b. Empty set
   c. Abelian P-root group
   d. AKS primality test

9. In mathematics, the _____ of two sets A and B is the set that contains all elements of A that also belong to B (or equivalently, all elements of B that also belong to A), but no other elements.

Chapter 1. Prerequisites

For explanation of the symbols used in this article, refer to the table of mathematical symbols.

The _____ of A and B

The _____ of A and B is written 'A ∩ B'.

a. AKS primality test
b. ADE classification
c. Abelian P-root group
d. Intersection

10. In geometry, a _____ is a straight curve. When geometry is used to model the real world, lines are used to represent straight objects with negligible width and height. Lines are an idealisation of such objects and have no width or height at all and are usually considered to be infinitely long.

a. -module
b. -equivalence
c. Line
d. 2-bridge knot

11. In set theory, the term _____ refers to a set operation used in the convergence of set elements to form a resultant set containing the elements of both sets. As a simple example, a _____ of two disjoint sets, which do not have elements in common results in a set containing all elements from both sets. A Venn diagram representing the _____ of sets A and B. If one circle represents A, and the other B, then the red area represents the _____ of A and B. The area where the circles join, also shown in red, is the intersection of the two sets.

If we define two sets which contain unique elements; those of A not occurring in B and vice versa, then the _____ of these sets results in a set which contains all elements of A and B. In terms of notation, we could define this set operation as the following:

A = {1,2,3,4}
B = {5,6,7,8}
$$A \cup B = \{1, 2, 3, 4, 5, 6, 7, 8\}$$

Other more complex operations can be done including the _____, if the set is for example defined by a property rather than a finite or assumed infinite enumeration of elements.

a. ADE classification
b. Union
c. Abelian P-root group
d. AKS primality test

12. In mathematics, an _____ is the finite or bounded case of a conic section, the geometric shape that results from cutting a circular conical or cylindrical surface with an oblique plane . It is also the locus of all points of the plane whose distances to two fixed points add to the same constant.

Ellipses also arise as images of a circle or a sphere under parallel projection, and some cases of perspective projection.

a. Abelian P-root group
b. Ellipse
c. ADE classification
d. AKS primality test

13. In mathematics, the _____ of a real number is its numerical value without regard to its sign. So, for example, 3 is the _____ of both 3 and −3.

The _____ of a number a is denoted by $|a|$.

a. ADE classification
b. Absolute value
c. Abelian P-root group
d. AKS primality test

14. In mathematics, a _____ of a number x is any number which, when repeatedly multiplied by itself, eventually yields x:

$$r \times r \times \cdots \times r = x.$$

In terms of exponentiation, r is a _____ of x if

$$r^n = x$$

for some positive integer n. For example, 2 is a _____ of 16 since $2^4 = 2 \times 2 \times 2 \times 2 = 16$.

The number n is called the degree of the _____.

a. Difference of two squares
b. Cubic function
c. Rationalisation
d. Root

15. The _____ of a Lie algebra $\mathfrak{g}$ is a particular ideal of $\mathfrak{g}$.

Let $\mathfrak{g}$ be a Lie algebra. The _____ of $\mathfrak{g}$ is defined as the largest solvable ideal of $\mathfrak{g}$.

a. Class sum
b. Cyclically reduced word
c. Garside element
d. Radical

16. In mathematics, a _____ of a number x is a number r such that r^2 = x, or, in other words, a number r whose square (the result of multiplying the number by itself) is x.

Every non-negative real number x has a unique non-negative _____, called the principal _____, which is denoted with a radical symbol as $\sqrt{x}$, or, using exponent notation, as $x^{1/2}$. For example, the principal _____ of 9 is 3, denoted $\sqrt{9} = 3$, because 3^2 = 3 × 3 = 9.

a. -equivalence
b. -module
c. 2-bridge knot
d. Square root

17. In elementary algebra, a _____ is a polynomial with two terms--the sum of two monomials--often bound by parenthesis or brackets when operated upon. It is the simplest kind of polynomial other than monomials.

- The _____ $a^2 - b^2$ can be factored as the product of two other binomials:

    $a^2 - b^2 = (a + b)(a - b.)$

    This is a special case of the more general formula:

    $$a^{n+1} - b^{n+1} = (a - b) \sum_{k=0}^{n} a^k b^{n-k}$$

- The product of a pair of linear binomials $(ax + b)$ and $(cx + d)$ is:

    $(ax + b)(cx + d) = acx^2 + axd + bcx + bd.$

- A _____ raised to the nth power, represented as

    $(a + b)^n$

    can be expanded by means of the _____ theorem or, equivalently, using Pascal's triangle. Taking a simple example, the perfect square _____ $(p + q)^2$ can be found by squaring the first digit, adding twice the product of the first and second digit and finally adding the square of the second digit, to give $p^2 + 2pq + q^2$.

a. Content
b. Generalized arithmetic progression
c. Theory of equations
d. Binomial

18. In mathematics, the word _____ is a term for any well-formed combination of mathematical symbols. For example,

   $x^2 + 3x - 4$

is an _____, while

   $)x) / 0$

is not, because the parentheses are not balanced and division by zero is undefined.

Being an _____ is a syntactic concept - the meaning of the variables is irrelevant, but different fields have different notions of validity.â€¢See formal language for how expressions are constructed, and formal semantics for meaning.

a. Arity
b. Unit ring
c. Orthogonal
d. Expression

19. In mathematics, the word _____ means two different things in the context of polynomials:

- The first meaning is a product of powers of variables, or formally any value obtained from 1 by finitely many multiplications by a variable. If only a single variable x is considered this means that any _____ is either 1 or a power x^n of x, with n a positive integer. If several variables are considered, say, x, y, z, then each can be given an exponent, so that any _____ is of the form $x^a y^b z^c$ with a,b,c nonnegative integers (taking note that any exponent 0 makes the corresponding factor equal to 1.)
- The second meaning of _____ includes monomials in the first sense, but also allows multiplication by any constant, so that $-7x^5$ and $(3 - 4i)x^4 yz^{13}$ are also considered to be monomials (the second example assuming polynomials in x, y, z over the complex numbers are considered.)

With either definition, the set of monomials is a subset of all polynomials that is closed under multiplication.

Both uses of this notion can be found, and in many cases the distinction is simply ignored, see for instance examples for the first and second meaning, and an unclear definition. In informal discussions the distinction is seldom important, and tendency is towards the broader second meaning. When studying the structure of polynomials however, one often definitely needs a notion with the first meaning.

a. Power sum symmetric polynomial
b. Schur polynomials
c. Monomial
d. Diagonal form

20. In elementary algebra, a _____ is a polynomial consisting of three terms; in other words, a _____ is the sum of three monomials. It can be factored using simple steps.

In linguistics, a _____ is a fixed expression which is made from three words; e.g. 'lights, camera, action', 'signed, sealed, delivered'.

a. Finitary operation
b. Polynomial Diophantine equation
c. Trinomial
d. Hall polynomials

Chapter 1. Prerequisites

21. A _____ is a symbol that stands for a value that may vary; the term usually occurs in opposition to constant, which is a symbol for a non-varying value, i.e. completely fixed or fixed in the context of use. The concepts of constants and variables are fundamental to all modern mathematics, science, engineering, and computer programming.

Much of the basic theory for which we use variables today, such as school geometry and algebra, was developed thousands of years ago, but the use of symbolic formulae and variables is only several hundreds of years old.

a. Variable
b. -module
c. 2-bridge knot
d. -equivalence

22. In mathematics, there are several meanings of _____ depending on the subject.

A _____, usually denoted by ° (the _____ symbol), is a measurement of plane angle, representing $\frac{1}{360}$ of a full rotation. When that angle is with respect to a reference meridian, it indicates a location along a great circle of a sphere, such as Earth , Mars, or the celestial sphere.

a. Degree
b. Median algebra
c. Relation algebra
d. Symmetric difference

23. When a polynomial is expressed as a sum or difference of terms (e.g., in standard or canonical form), the exponent of the term with the highest exponent is the _____. The degree of a term is the sum of the powers of each variable in the term. The words degree and order are used interchangeably.

a. Secondary polynomials
b. Degree of the polynomial
c. Multivariate division algorithm
d. Lommel polynomial

24. _____ is one of the four basic arithmetic operations; it is the inverse of addition, meaning that if we start with any number and add any number and then subtract the same number we added, we return to the number we started with. _____ is denoted by a minus sign in infix notation.

The traditional names for the parts of the formula

$c - b = a$

are minuend (c) − subtrahend (b) = difference (a.)

a. 2-bridge knot
b. -module
c. Subtraction
d. -equivalence

25. In mathematics, _____(F_n) is the outer automorphism group of a free group on n generators. These groups play an important role in geometric group theory.

_____(F_n) acts geometrically on a cell complex known as outer space, which can be thought of as the Teichmüller space for a bouquet of circles.

a. AKS primality test
b. Out
c. Abelian P-root group
d. ADE classification

26. A _____ is a three-dimensional solid object bounded by six square faces, facets or sides, with three meeting at each vertex. The _____ can also be called a regular hexahedron and is one of the five Platonic solids. It is a special kind of square prism, of rectangular parallelepiped and of trigonal trapezohedron.

a. -equivalence
b. -module
c. 2-bridge knot
d. Cube

27. In mathematics, especially in the area of abstract algebra known as ring theory, a _____ is a ring with 0 ≠ 1 such that ab = 0 implies that either a = 0 or b = 0 (the zero-product property.) That is, it is a nontrivial ring without left or right zero divisors. A commutative _____ is called an integral _____.

a. Partially-ordered ring
b. Coherent ring
c. Subring
d. Domain

28. In algebra, a _____ of an element in a quadratic extension field of a field K is its image under the unique non-identity automorphism of the extended field that fixes K. If the extension is generated by a square root of an element r of K, then the _____ of $a + b\sqrt{r}$ is $a - b\sqrt{r}$ for $a, b \in K$, and in particular in the case of the field C of complex numbers as an extension of the field R of real numbers (where r = − 1), the complex _____ of a + bi is a − bi.

Forming the sum or product of any element of the extension field with its _____ always gives an element of K. This can be used to rewrite a quotient of numbers in the extended field so that the denominator lies in K, by multiplying numerator and denominator by the _____ of the denominator. This process is called rationalization of the denominator, in particular if K is the field Q of rational numbers.

a. K-theory
b. Digital root
c. Field arithmetic
d. Conjugate

12 **Chapter 2. Equations and Inequalities**

1. In mathematics, an _____ represents a solution, such as that to an equation, that emerges from the process of solving the problem but is not a valid solution to the original problem. A missing solution is a solution that was a valid solution to the original problem, but disappeared during the process of solving the problem. Both are frequently the consequence of performing operations that are not invertible for some or all values of the variables, which disturbs the chain of logical implications in the proof.

   a. Unary operation
   b. Unitary method
   c. Equating the coefficients
   d. Extraneous solution

2. The _____ of a Lie algebra $\mathfrak{g}$ is a particular ideal of $\mathfrak{g}$.

   Let $\mathfrak{g}$ be a Lie algebra. The _____ of $\mathfrak{g}$ is defined as the largest solvable ideal of $\mathfrak{g}$.

   a. Class sum
   b. Cyclically reduced word
   c. Garside element
   d. Radical

3. In mathematics, a _____ of a number x is any number which, when repeatedly multiplied by itself, eventually yields x:

   $$r \times r \times \cdots \times r = x.$$

   In terms of exponentiation, r is a _____ of x if

   $$r^n = x$$

   for some positive integer n. For example, 2 is a _____ of 16 since $2^4 = 2 \times 2 \times 2 \times 2 = 16$.

   The number n is called the degree of the _____.

   a. Cubic function
   b. Difference of two squares
   c. Rationalisation
   d. Root

4. A _____ is a symbol that stands for a value that may vary; the term usually occurs in opposition to constant, which is a symbol for a non-varying value, i.e. completely fixed or fixed in the context of use. The concepts of constants and variables are fundamental to all modern mathematics, science, engineering, and computer programming.

Chapter 2. Equations and Inequalities

Much of the basic theory for which we use variables today, such as school geometry and algebra, was developed thousands of years ago, but the use of symbolic formulae and variables is only several hundreds of years old.

a. Variable
b. 2-bridge knot
c. -equivalence
d. -module

5. In mathematics, the term _____ is used to describe an algebraic structures which in some sense cannot be divided by a smaller structure of the same type. Put another way, an algebraic structure is _____ if the kernel of every homomorphism is either the whole structure or a single element. Some examples are:

- A group is called a _____ group if it does not contain a non-trivial proper normal subgroup.
- A ring is called a _____ ring if it does not contain a non-trivial two sided ideal.
- A module is called a _____ module if does not contain a non-trivial submodule.
- An algebra is called a _____ algebra if does not contain a non-trivial two sided ideal.

The general pattern is that the structure admits no non-trivial congruence relations.

a. Commutativity
b. Linear combinations
c. Polarization identity
d. Simple

6. In mathematics, a _____ is a polynomial equation of the second degree. The general form is

$$ax^2 + bx + c = 0$$

The quadratic coefficient a is the coefficient of x^2, the linear coefficient b is the coefficient of x, and c is the constant coefficient, also called the free term or constant term.

Quadratic equations are called quadratic because the variable in the leading term is squared.

a. Rationalisation
b. Cubic function
c. Difference of two squares
d. Quadratic equation

7. In mathematics, a _____ or quadratic is a polynomial of degree two. A _____ may involve a single variable x, or multiple variables such as x, y, and z.

Any single-variable _____ may be written as

$$ax^2 + bx + c,$$

where x is the variable, and a, b, and c represent the coefficients.

   a. Polynomial remainder theorem
   b. Quadratic polynomial
   c. Sheffer sequence
   d. Littlewood polynomial

8. In mathematics, the _____ of a real number is its numerical value without regard to its sign. So, for example, 3 is the _____ of both 3 and −3.

The _____ of a number a is denoted by $|a|$.

   a. ADE classification
   b. AKS primality test
   c. Abelian P-root group
   d. Absolute value

9. In elementary algebra, _____ is a technique for converting a quadratic polynomial of the form

$$ax^2 + bx + c$$

to the form

$$a(\cdots\cdots)^2 + \text{constant}.$$

The expression inside the parenthesis is of the form x − constant. Thus one converts $ax^2 + bx + c$ to

$$a(x - h)^2 + k$$

and one must find h and k.

_____ is used in

- solving quadratic equations,
- graphing quadratic functions,
- evaluating integrals in calculus,
- finding Laplace transforms.

In mathematics, _____ is considered a basic algebraic operation, and is often applied without remark in any computation involving quadratic polynomials.

There is a simple formula in elementary algebra for computing the square of a binomial:

$$(x+p)^2 = x^2 + 2px + p^2.$$

For example:

$$(x+3)^2 = x^2 + 6x + 9 \qquad (p=3)$$
$$(x-5)^2 = x^2 - 10x + 25 \qquad (p=-5).$$

In any perfect square, the number p is always half the coefficient of x, and then the constant term is equal to p^2.

a. Content
b. Reduct
c. Nested radical
d. Completing the square

10. In algebra, the _____ of a polynomial with real or complex coefficients is a certain expression in the coefficients of the polynomial which is a symmetric polynomial in the coefficients and gives information on the nature of the roots; in particular, it is equal to zero if and only if the polynomial has a multiple root (i.e. a root with multiplicity greater than one) in the complex numbers. For example, the _____ of the quadratic polynomial

$$ax^2 + bx + c \text{ is } b^2 - 4ac.$$

The _____ of the cubic polynomial

$$ax^3 + bx^2 + cx + d \text{ is } b^2c^2 - 4ac^3 - 4b^3d - 27a^2d^2 + 18abcd.$$

a. Polynomial remainder theorem
b. Kazhdan-Lusztig polynomials
c. Discriminant
d. Minimal polynomial

11. In mathematics, the complex numbers are an extension of the real numbers obtained by adjoining an imaginary unit, denoted i, which satisfies:

$$i^2 = -1.$$

Every _____ can be written in the form a + bi, where a and b are real numbers called the real part and the imaginary part of the _____, respectively.

Complex numbers are a field, and thus have addition, subtraction, multiplication, and division operations. These operations extend the corresponding operations on real numbers, although with a number of additional elegant and useful properties, e.g., negative real numbers can be obtained by squaring complex (imaginary) numbers.

a. 2-bridge knot
b. Complex number
c. -module
d. -equivalence

12. In mathematics, an _____ is a complex number whose squared value is a real number less than or equal to zero. The imaginary unit, denoted by i or j, is an example of an _____. If y is a real number, then i·y is an _____, because:

$$(i \cdot y)^2 = i^2 \cdot y^2 = -y^2 \leq 0.$$

Imaginary numbers were defined in 1572 by Rafael Bombelli.

a. AKS primality test
b. ADE classification
c. Abelian P-root group
d. Imaginary number

13. _____ is the mathematical process of putting things together. The plus sign '+' means that numbers are added together. For example, in the picture on the right, there are 3 + 2 apples--meaning three apples and two other apples--which is the same as five apples, since 3 + 2 = 5.

a. AKS primality test
b. Abelian P-root group
c. Addition
d. ADE classification

14. In algebra, a commutative ring R is said to be _____ if any of the following equivalent conditions holds:

   1. The localization $R_\mathfrak{m}$ of R at $\mathfrak{m}$ is a valuation ring for every maximal ideal $\mathfrak{m}$ of R.
   2. For all ideals $\mathfrak{a}$, $\mathfrak{b}$, and $\mathfrak{c}$,

$$\mathfrak{a} \cap (\mathfrak{b} + \mathfrak{c}) = (\mathfrak{a} \cap \mathfrak{b}) + (\mathfrak{a} \cap \mathfrak{c})$$

- For all ideals $\mathfrak{a}$, $\mathfrak{b}$, and $\mathfrak{c}$,

$$\mathfrak{a} + (\mathfrak{b} \cap \mathfrak{c}) = (\mathfrak{a} + \mathfrak{b}) \cap (\mathfrak{a} + \mathfrak{c})$$

An _____ domain is called a Prüfer domain.

a. Ordered vector space
b. Arithmetical
c. Inverse eigenvalues theorem
d. Exchange matrix

15. In its simplest meaning in mathematics and logic, an _____ is an action or procedure which produces a new value from one or more input values. There are two common types of operations: unary and binary. Unary operations involve only one value, such as negation and trigonometric functions.
a. Operation
b. Abelian P-root group
c. ADE classification
d. AKS primality test

16. In mathematics, the (formal) _____ of a complex vector space V is the complex vector space $\overline{V}$ consisting of all formal complex conjugates of elements of V. That is, $\overline{V}$ is a vector space whose elements are in one-to-one correspondence with the elements of V:

$$\overline{V} = \{\overline{v} \mid v \in V\},$$

with the following rules for addition and scalar multiplication:

$$\overline{v} + \overline{w} = \overline{v+w} \quad \text{and} \quad \alpha\overline{v} = \overline{\overline{\alpha}v}.$$

Here v and w are vectors in V, α is a complex number, and $\overline{\alpha}$ denotes the _____ of α.

In the case where V is a linear subspace of $\mathbb{C}^n$, the formal _____ $\overline{V}$ is naturally isomorphic to the actual _____ subspace of V in $\mathbb{C}^n$.

  a. Conjugate transpose
  b. Polynomial basis
  c. Binomial inverse theorem
  d. Complex conjugate

17. In algebra, a _____ of an element in a quadratic extension field of a field K is its image under the unique non-identity automorphism of the extended field that fixes K. If the extension is generated by a square root of an element r of K, then the _____ of $a + b\sqrt{r}$ is $a - b\sqrt{r}$ for $a, b \in K$, and in particular in the case of the field C of complex numbers as an extension of the field R of real numbers (where r = − 1), the complex _____ of a + bi is a − bi.

Forming the sum or product of any element of the extension field with its _____ always gives an element of K. This can be used to rewrite a quotient of numbers in the extended field so that the denominator lies in K, by multiplying numerator and denominator by the _____ of the denominator. This process is called rationalization of the denominator, in particular if K is the field Q of rational numbers.

  a. K-theory
  b. Field arithmetic
  c. Digital root
  d. Conjugate

18. In mathematics, especially in elementary arithmetic, _____ is an arithmetic operation which is the inverse of multiplication.

Specifically, if c times b equals a, written:

$$c \times b = a$$

where b is not zero, then a divided by b equals c, written:

$$\frac{a}{b} = c$$

For instance,

$$\frac{6}{3} = 2$$

since

$$2 \times 3 = 6.$$

In the above expression, a is called the dividend, b the divisor and c the quotient.

   a. Division
   b. 2-bridge knot
   c. -equivalence
   d. -module

19. In mathematics, a _____ of a number x is a number r such that r^2 = x, or, in other words, a number r whose square (the result of multiplying the number by itself) is x.

Every non-negative real number x has a unique non-negative _____, called the principal _____, which is denoted with a radical symbol as $\sqrt{x}$, or, using exponent notation, as $x^{1/2}$. For example, the principal _____ of 9 is 3, denoted $\sqrt{9} = 3$, because 3^2 = 3 × 3 = 9.

   a. 2-bridge knot
   b. Square root
   c. -module
   d. -equivalence

20. In mathematics, an _____ is a statement about the relative size or order of two objects, or about whether they are the same or not

- The notation a < b means that a is less than b.
- The notation a > b means that a is greater than b.
- The notation a ≠ b means that a is not equal to b, but does not say that one is bigger than the other or even that they can be compared in size.

In all these cases, a is not equal to b, hence, '_____'.

These relations are known as strict _____

- The notation a ≤ b means that a is less than or equal to b (or, equivalently, not greater than b);
- The notation a ≥ b means that a is greater than or equal to b (or, equivalently, not smaller than b);

An additional use of the notation is to show that one quantity is much greater than another, normally by several orders of magnitude.

- The notation a ≪ b means that a is much less than b.
- The notation a ≫ b means that a is much greater than b.

If the sense of the _____ is the same for all values of the variables for which its members are defined, then the _____ is called an 'absolute' or 'unconditional' _____. If the sense of an _____ holds only for certain values of the variables involved, but is reversed or destroyed for other values of the variables, it is called a conditional _____.

One can apply the same algebraic operations to inequalities as one would apply for solving equalities. For example, to find x for the _____ 10x > 20 one would divide 20 by 10 to obtain x > 2.

a. Inequality
b. ADE classification
c. Abelian P-root group
d. AKS primality test

21. In mathematics a _____ is an inequality which involves a linear function.

When operating in terms of real numbers, linear inequalities are the ones written in the forms

f(x) < b or $f(x) \leq b$,

Chapter 2. Equations and Inequalities

where f(x) is a linear functional in real numbers and b is a constant real number. Alternatively, these may be viewed as

g(x) < 0 or $g(x) \leq 0$,

where g(x) is an affine function.

a. Linear inequality
b. Flag
c. Semi-simple operators
d. Fundamental theorem of linear algebra

22. In group theory, a branch of mathematics, the term _____ is used in two closely related senses:

- the _____ of a group is its cardinality, i.e. the number of its elements;
- the _____, sometimes period, of an element a of a group is the smallest positive integer m such that a^m = e (where e denotes the identity element of the group, and a^m denotes the product of m copies of a.) If no such m exists, we say that a has infinite _____. All elements of finite groups have finite _____.

We denote the _____ of a group G by ord(G) or $|G|$ and the _____ of an element a by ord(a) or $|a|$.

Example. The symmetric group S_3 has the following multiplication table.

This group has six elements, so ord(S_3) = 6.

a. Artin group
b. Index calculus algorithm
c. Outer automorphism group
d. Order

Chapter 3. Coordinates and Graphs

1. In mathematics, a _____ is a flat surface. Planes can arise as subspaces of some higher dimensional space, as with the walls of a room, or they may enjoy an independent existence in their own right, as in the setting of Euclidean geometry
    a. Similarity
    b. -equivalence
    c. -module
    d. Plane

2. In mathematics, a (B, N) _____ is a structure on groups of Lie type that allows one to give uniform proofs of many results, instead of giving a large number of case-by-case proofs. Roughly speaking, it shows that all such groups are similar to the general linear group over a field. They were invented by the mathematician Jacques Tits, and are also sometimes known as Tits systems.
    a. Pair
    b. Rank of a group
    c. Group action
    d. Group representations

3. In geometry, a _____ is a straight curve. When geometry is used to model the real world, lines are used to represent straight objects with negligible width and height. Lines are an idealisation of such objects and have no width or height at all and are usually considered to be infinitely long.
    a. 2-bridge knot
    b. -module
    c. -equivalence
    d. Line

4. In mathematics, an _____ is the finite or bounded case of a conic section, the geometric shape that results from cutting a circular conical or cylindrical surface with an oblique plane . It is also the locus of all points of the plane whose distances to two fixed points add to the same constant.

Ellipses also arise as images of a circle or a sphere under parallel projection, and some cases of perspective projection.

   a. ADE classification
   b. AKS primality test
   c. Abelian P-root group
   d. Ellipse

Chapter 3. Coordinates and Graphs

5. _____, usually called coordinate geometry and earlier referred to as Cartesian geometry or analytical geometry, is the study of geometry using the principles of algebra; the modern development of _____ is thus suggestively called algebraic geometry.

Usually the Cartesian coordinate system is applied to manipulate equations for planes, straight lines, and squares, often in two and sometimes in three dimensions of measurement. Geometrical, one studies the Euclidean plane (2 dimensions) and Euclidean space (3 dimensions.)

   a. AKS primality test
   b. Analytic Geometry
   c. Enumerative geometry
   d. ADE classification

6. A _____ is a symbol that stands for a value that may vary; the term usually occurs in opposition to constant, which is a symbol for a non-varying value, i.e. completely fixed or fixed in the context of use. The concepts of constants and variables are fundamental to all modern mathematics, science, engineering, and computer programming.

Much of the basic theory for which we use variables today, such as school geometry and algebra, was developed thousands of years ago, but the use of symbolic formulae and variables is only several hundreds of years old.

   a. 2-bridge knot
   b. -module
   c. -equivalence
   d. Variable

7. In mathematics, an _____ is a statement about the relative size or order of two objects, or about whether they are the same or not

   - The notation a < b means that a is less than b.
   - The notation a > b means that a is greater than b.
   - The notation a ≠ b means that a is not equal to b, but does not say that one is bigger than the other or even that they can be compared in size.

In all these cases, a is not equal to b, hence, '_____'.

These relations are known as strict _____

   - The notation a ≤ b means that a is less than or equal to b (or, equivalently, not greater than b);
   - The notation a ≥ b means that a is greater than or equal to b (or, equivalently, not smaller than b);

An additional use of the notation is to show that one quantity is much greater than another, normally by several orders of magnitude.

- The notation a ≉ b means that a is much less than b.
- The notation a ≉ b means that a is much greater than b.

If the sense of the _____ is the same for all values of the variables for which its members are defined, then the _____ is called an 'absolute' or 'unconditional' _____. If the sense of an _____ holds only for certain values of the variables involved, but is reversed or destroyed for other values of the variables, it is called a conditional _____.

One can apply the same algebraic operations to inequalities as one would apply for solving equalities. For example, to find x for the _____ 10x > 20 one would divide 20 by 10 to obtain x > 2.

a. Inequality
b. Abelian P-root group
c. ADE classification
d. AKS primality test

8. In geometry, two lines or planes (or a line and a plane), are considered _____ to each other if they form congruent adjacent angles (an L-shape.) The term may be used as a noun or adjective. Thus, referring to Figure 1, the line AB is the _____ to CD through the point B. Note that by definition, a line is infinitely long, and strictly speaking AB and CD in this example represent line segments of two infinitely long lines.
a. Perpendicular
b. 2-bridge knot
c. -module
d. -equivalence

9. In geometry, a _____ is a surface of revolution in the shape of a helix with thickness, generated by revolving a circle about the path of a helix. The torus is a special case of the _____ obtained when the helix is crushed to a circle.

A _____ wrapped around the z-axis can be defined parametrically by:

$$x(u,v) = (R + r\cos v)\cos u,$$
$$y(u,v) = (R + r\cos v)\sin u,$$
$$z(u,v) = r\sin v + \frac{P \cdot u}{\pi},$$

where

$$u \in [0,\ 2n\pi] \ (n \in \mathbb{R}),$$
$$v \in [0,\ 2\pi],$$

R is the distance from the center of the tube to the center of the helix,
r is the radius of the tube,
P is the speed of the movement along the z axis (in a right-handed Cartesian coordinate system, positive values create right-handed springs, whereas negative values create left-handed springs),
n is the number of rounds in circle.

a. Ruled surfaces
b. PDE surfaces
c. Steiner surfaces
d. Spring

10. The most commonly encountered form of Hooke's law is probably the spring equation, which relates the force exerted by a spring to the distance it is stretched by a _____, k, measured in force per length.

$$F = -kx$$

The negative sign indicates that the force exerted by the spring is in direct opposition to the direction of displacement. It is called a 'restoring force', as it tends to restore the system to equilibrium.

a. 2-bridge knot
b. Spring constant
c. -module
d. -equivalence

11. In mathematics, a _____ is a constant multiplicative factor of a certain object. For example, in the expression $9x^2$, the _____ of x^2 is 9.

The object can be such things as a variable, a vector, a function, etc.

a. Constant term
b. Coefficient
c. Tschirnhaus transformation
d. Vandermonde polynomial

Chapter 4. Functions

1. An _____ is a pointed projectile that is shot with a bow. It predates recorded history and is common to most cultures. Schematic of an _____ with many parts.

A normal _____ consists of a shaft with an arrowhead attached to the front end, with fletchings and a nock at the other.

   a. Arrow
   b. AKS primality test
   c. Abelian P-root group
   d. ADE classification

2. In mathematics, especially in the area of abstract algebra known as ring theory, a _____ is a ring with 0 ≠ 1 such that ab = 0 implies that either a = 0 or b = 0 (the zero-product property.) That is, it is a nontrivial ring without left or right zero divisors. A commutative _____ is called an integral _____.
   a. Domain
   b. Coherent ring
   c. Subring
   d. Partially-ordered ring

3. A _____ is a symbol that stands for a value that may vary; the term usually occurs in opposition to constant, which is a symbol for a non-varying value, i.e. completely fixed or fixed in the context of use. The concepts of constants and variables are fundamental to all modern mathematics, science, engineering, and computer programming.

Much of the basic theory for which we use variables today, such as school geometry and algebra, was developed thousands of years ago, but the use of symbolic formulae and variables is only several hundreds of years old.

   a. 2-bridge knot
   b. Variable
   c. -equivalence
   d. -module

4. In mathematics, the word _____ is a term for any well-formed combination of mathematical symbols. For example,

$$x^2 + 3x - 4$$

is an _____, while

$$)x) / 0$$

is not, because the parentheses are not balanced and division by zero is undefined.

Being an _____ is a syntactic concept - the meaning of the variables is irrelevant, but different fields have different notions of validity.â€See formal language for how expressions are constructed, and formal semantics for meaning.

a. Orthogonal
b. Unit ring
c. Arity
d. Expression

5. In mathematics, an _____ is the finite or bounded case of a conic section, the geometric shape that results from cutting a circular conical or cylindrical surface with an oblique plane . It is also the locus of all points of the plane whose distances to two fixed points add to the same constant.

Ellipses also arise as images of a circle or a sphere under parallel projection, and some cases of perspective projection.

a. Ellipse
b. Abelian P-root group
c. ADE classification
d. AKS primality test

6. In mathematics, the _____ of a real number is its numerical value without regard to its sign. So, for example, 3 is the _____ of both 3 and −3.

The _____ of a number a is denoted by $|a|$.

a. AKS primality test
b. Absolute value
c. Abelian P-root group
d. ADE classification

7. The _____ are natural numbers including 0 ' href='/wiki/0_(number)'>0, 1, 2, 3, ...) and their negatives (0, −1, −2, −3, ...). They are numbers that can be written without a fractional or decimal component, and fall within the set {...

a. AKS primality test
b. Abelian P-root group
c. ADE classification
d. Integers

8. In geometry, a _____ is a straight curve. When geometry is used to model the real world, lines are used to represent straight objects with negligible width and height. Lines are an idealisation of such objects and have no width or height at all and are usually considered to be infinitely long.
   a. -module
   b. Line
   c. -equivalence
   d. 2-bridge knot

9. In mathematics, a _____ of a number x is any number which, when repeatedly multiplied by itself, eventually yields x:

$$r \times r \times \cdots \times r = x.$$

In terms of exponentiation, r is a _____ of x if

$$r^n = x$$

for some positive integer n. For example, 2 is a _____ of 16 since 2^4 = 2 × 2 × 2 × 2 = 16.

The number n is called the degree of the _____.

   a. Difference of two squares
   b. Rationalisation
   c. Cubic function
   d. Root

10. In mathematics, an _____ is a statement about the relative size or order of two objects, or about whether they are the same or not

   - The notation a < b means that a is less than b.
   - The notation a > b means that a is greater than b.
   - The notation a ≠ b means that a is not equal to b, but does not say that one is bigger than the other or even that they can be compared in size.

Chapter 4. Functions

In all these cases, a is not equal to b, hence, '_____'.

These relations are known as strict _____

- The notation a ≤ b means that a is less than or equal to b (or, equivalently, not greater than b);
- The notation a ≥ b means that a is greater than or equal to b (or, equivalently, not smaller than b);

An additional use of the notation is to show that one quantity is much greater than another, normally by several orders of magnitude.

- The notation a ≪ b means that a is much less than b.
- The notation a ≫ b means that a is much greater than b.

If the sense of the _____ is the same for all values of the variables for which its members are defined, then the _____ is called an 'absolute' or 'unconditional' _____. If the sense of an _____ holds only for certain values of the variables involved, but is reversed or destroyed for other values of the variables, it is called a conditional _____.

One can apply the same algebraic operations to inequalities as one would apply for solving equalities. For example, to find x for the _____ 10x > 20 one would divide 20 by 10 to obtain x > 2.

a. Abelian P-root group
b. Inequality
c. AKS primality test
d. ADE classification

11. In mathematics a _____ is an inequality which involves a linear function.

When operating in terms of real numbers, linear inequalities are the ones written in the forms

$$f(x) < b \text{ or } f(x) \leq b,$$

where f(x) is a linear functional in real numbers and b is a constant real number. Alternatively, these may be viewed as

$$g(x) < 0 \text{ or } g(x) \leq 0,$$

where g(x) is an affine function.

a. Semi-simple operators
b. Flag
c. Fundamental theorem of linear algebra
d. Linear Inequality

12. A _____, in mathematics, is a polynomial function of the form f(x) = ax² + bx + c = 0, where $a \neq 0$. The graph of a _____ is a parabola whose major axis is parallel to the y-axis.

The expression ax² + bx + c in the definition of a _____ is a polynomial of degree 2 or second order, or a 2nd degree polynomial, because the highest exponent of x is 2.

a. Factor theorem
b. Vandermonde polynomial
c. Dickson polynomials
d. Quadratic function

13. In elementary algebra, _____ is a technique for converting a quadratic polynomial of the form

$$ax^2 + bx + c$$

to the form

$$a(\cdots\cdots)^2 + \text{constant}.$$

The expression inside the parenthesis is of the form x − constant. Thus one converts ax² + bx + c to

$$a(x - h)^2 + k$$

and one must find h and k.

_____ is used in

- solving quadratic equations,
- graphing quadratic functions,
- evaluating integrals in calculus,
- finding Laplace transforms.

In mathematics, _____ is considered a basic algebraic operation, and is often applied without remark in any computation involving quadratic polynomials.

There is a simple formula in elementary algebra for computing the square of a binomial:

$$(x+p)^2 = x^2 + 2px + p^2.$$

For example:

$$(x+3)^2 = x^2 + 6x + 9 \quad (p=3)$$
$$(x-5)^2 = x^2 - 10x + 25 \quad (p=-5).$$

In any perfect square, the number p is always half the coefficient of x, and then the constant term is equal to p^2.

   a. Content
   b. Completing the square
   c. Nested radical
   d. Reduct

14. In mathematics, the _____ is a conic section, the intersection of a right circular conical surface and a plane parallel to a generating straight line of that surface. Given a point (the focus) and a line (the directrix) that lie in a plane, the locus of points in that plane that are equidistant to them is a _____.

A particular case arises when the plane is tangent to the conical surface of a circle.

   a. -equivalence
   b. Parabola
   c. 2-bridge knot
   d. -module

15. In a totally ordered set all elements are mutually comparable, so such a set can have at most one minimal element and at most one maximal element. Then, due to mutual comparability, the minimal element will also be the least element and the maximal element will also be the greatest element. Thus in a totally ordered set we can simply use the terms _____ and maximum.

   a. -equivalence
   b. 2-bridge knot
   c. -module
   d. Minimum

Chapter 4. Functions

16. A _____ is a three-dimensional solid object bounded by six square faces, facets or sides, with three meeting at each vertex. The _____ can also be called a regular hexahedron and is one of the five Platonic solids. It is a special kind of square prism, of rectangular parallelepiped and of trigonal trapezohedron.
    a. -equivalence
    b. -module
    c. Cube
    d. 2-bridge knot

17. _____ is the mathematical process of putting things together. The plus sign '+' means that numbers are added together. For example, in the picture on the right, there are 3 + 2 apples--meaning three apples and two other apples--which is the same as five apples, since 3 + 2 = 5.
    a. ADE classification
    b. Abelian P-root group
    c. AKS primality test
    d. Addition

18. In mathematics, a _____ represents the application of one function to the results of another. For instance, the functions f: X → Y and g: Y → Z can be composed by first computing f(x) and then applying a function g to the output of f(x.)

    Thus one obtains a function g ∘ f: X → Z defined by (g ∘ f)(x) = g(f(x)) for all x in X. The notation g ∘ f is read as 'g circle f', or 'g composed with f', 'g after f', 'g following f', or just 'g of f'.

    a. Linear map
    b. Shear mappings
    c. Reflection
    d. Composite function

19. A _____ or logistic curve is the most common sigmoid curve. It models the S-curve of growth of some set P, where P might be thought of as population. The initial stage of growth is approximately exponential; then, as saturation begins, the growth slows, and at maturity, growth stops.
    a. Lommel functions
    b. Logistic function
    c. Struve function
    d. Lambert W function

Chapter 5. Polynomial and Rational Functions

1. In mathematics, a _____ is a constant multiplicative factor of a certain object. For example, in the expression $9x^2$, the _____ of x^2 is 9.

The object can be such things as a variable, a vector, a function, etc.

   a. Coefficient
   b. Tschirnhaus transformation
   c. Constant term
   d. Vandermonde polynomial

2. In mathematics, the word _____ means two different things in the context of polynomials:

   - The first meaning is a product of powers of variables, or formally any value obtained from 1 by finitely many multiplications by a variable. If only a single variable x is considered this means that any _____ is either 1 or a power x^n of x, with n a positive integer. If several variables are considered, say, x, y, z, then each can be given an exponent, so that any _____ is of the form $x^a y^b z^c$ with a,b,c nonnegative integers (taking note that any exponent 0 makes the corresponding factor equal to 1.)
   - The second meaning of _____ includes monomials in the first sense, but also allows multiplication by any constant, so that $-7x^5$ and $(3 - 4i)x^4yz^{13}$ are also considered to be monomials (the second example assuming polynomials in x, y, z over the complex numbers are considered.)

With either definition, the set of monomials is a subset of all polynomials that is closed under multiplication.

Both uses of this notion can be found, and in many cases the distinction is simply ignored, see for instance examples for the first and second meaning, and an unclear definition. In informal discussions the distinction is seldom important, and tendency is towards the broader second meaning. When studying the structure of polynomials however, one often definitely needs a notion with the first meaning.

   a. Power sum symmetric polynomial
   b. Monomial
   c. Diagonal form
   d. Schur polynomials

3. In mathematics, an _____ is the finite or bounded case of a conic section, the geometric shape that results from cutting a circular conical or cylindrical surface with an oblique plane . It is also the locus of all points of the plane whose distances to two fixed points add to the same constant.

Ellipses also arise as images of a circle or a sphere under parallel projection, and some cases of perspective projection.

Chapter 5. Polynomial and Rational Functions

   a. Ellipse
   b. AKS primality test
   c. Abelian P-root group
   d. ADE classification

4. In mathematics, there are several meanings of _____ depending on the subject.

A _____, usually denoted by ° (the _____ symbol), is a measurement of plane angle, representing $1/360$ of a full rotation. When that angle is with respect to a reference meridian, it indicates a location along a great circle of a sphere, such as Earth, Mars, or the celestial sphere.

   a. Symmetric difference
   b. Median algebra
   c. Relation algebra
   d. Degree

5. When a polynomial is expressed as a sum or difference of terms (e.g., in standard or canonical form), the exponent of the term with the highest exponent is the _____. The degree of a term is the sum of the powers of each variable in the term. The words degree and order are used interchangeably.
   a. Secondary polynomials
   b. Degree of the polynomial
   c. Multivariate division algorithm
   d. Lommel polynomial

6. In a totally ordered set all elements are mutually comparable, so such a set can have at most one minimal element and at most one maximal element. Then, due to mutual comparability, the minimal element will also be the least element and the maximal element will also be the greatest element. Thus in a totally ordered set we can simply use the terms _____ and maximum.
   a. Minimum
   b. -module
   c. 2-bridge knot
   d. -equivalence

7. In mathematics, especially in elementary arithmetic, _____ is an arithmetic operation which is the inverse of multiplication.

Chapter 5. Polynomial and Rational Functions

Specifically, if c times b equals a, written:

$$c \times b = a$$

where b is not zero, then a divided by b equals c, written:

$$\frac{a}{b} = c$$

For instance,

$$\frac{6}{3} = 2$$

since

$$2 \times 3 = 6.$$

In the above expression, a is called the dividend, b the divisor and c the quotient.

   a. -module
   b. 2-bridge knot
   c. -equivalence
   d. Division

8. In mathematics, the complex numbers are an extension of the real numbers obtained by adjoining an imaginary unit, denoted i, which satisfies:

$$i^2 = -1.$$

Every _____ can be written in the form a + bi, where a and b are real numbers called the real part and the imaginary part of the _____, respectively.

Complex numbers are a field, and thus have addition, subtraction, multiplication, and division operations. These operations extend the corresponding operations on real numbers, although with a number of additional elegant and useful properties, e.g., negative real numbers can be obtained by squaring complex (imaginary) numbers.

a. 2-bridge knot
b. -module
c. -equivalence
d. Complex number

9. In algebraic geometry, divisors are a generalization of codimension one subvarieties of algebraic varieties; two different generalizations are in common use, Cartier divisors and Weil divisors The concepts agree on non-singular varieties over algebraically closed fields.

A Weil _____ is a locally finite linear combination (with integral coefficients) of irreducible subvarieties of codimension one.

a. Divisor
b. Picard group
c. Lefschetz pencil
d. Linear system of divisors

10. In algebra, the _____ is a theorem for finding out the factors of a polynomial (an expression in which the terms are only added, subtracted or multiplied, e.g. $x^2 + 6x + 6$.) It is a special case of the polynomial remainder theorem.

The _____ states that a polynomial f(x) has a factor x − k if and only if f(k) = 0.

a. Remez algorithm
b. Difference polynomial
c. Quadratic function
d. Factor Theorem

11. In mathematics, a _____ of a number x is any number which, when repeatedly multiplied by itself, eventually yields x:

$$r \times r \times \cdots \times r = x.$$

In terms of exponentiation, r is a _____ of x if

$$r^n = x$$

for some positive integer n. For example, 2 is a _____ of 16 since $2^4 = 2 \times 2 \times 2 \times 2 = 16$.

The number n is called the degree of the _____.

Chapter 5. Polynomial and Rational Functions

a. Difference of two squares
b. Cubic function
c. Rationalisation
d. Root

12. In mathematics, _____ or factoring is the decomposition of an object ' href='/wiki/Matrix_(mathematics)'>matrix) into a product of other objects, or factors, which when multiplied together give the original. For example, the number 15 factors into primes as 3 × 5, and the polynomial $x^2 - 4$ factors as (x − 2)(x + 2.) In all cases, a product of simpler objects is obtained.
    a. Factorization
    b. -module
    c. -equivalence
    d. 2-bridge knot

13. In algebra, a _____ of an element in a quadratic extension field of a field K is its image under the unique non-identity automorphism of the extended field that fixes K. If the extension is generated by a square root of an element r of K, then the _____ of $a + b\sqrt{r}$ is $a - b\sqrt{r}$ for $a, b \in K$, and in particular in the case of the field C of complex numbers as an extension of the field R of real numbers (where r = − 1), the complex _____ of a + bi is a − bi.

Forming the sum or product of any element of the extension field with its _____ always gives an element of K. This can be used to rewrite a quotient of numbers in the extended field so that the denominator lies in K, by multiplying numerator and denominator by the _____ of the denominator. This process is called rationalization of the denominator, in particular if K is the field Q of rational numbers.

   a. Field arithmetic
   b. Digital root
   c. K-theory
   d. Conjugate

14. In mathematics, the adjective _____ means that an object cannot be expressed as a product of more than one non-trivial factors in a given set. See also factorization.

For any field F, the ring of polynomials with coefficients in F is denoted by F[x].

a. Alternating polynomial
b. Integer-valued polynomial
c. Ehrhart polynomial
d. Irreducible

15. In mathematics, a _____ is any function which can be written as the ratio of two polynomial functions. _____ of degree 2 : $$y = \frac{x^2 - 3x - 2}{x^2 - 4}$$

In the case of one variable, x, a _____ is a function of the form

$$f(x) = \frac{P(x)}{Q(x)}$$

where P and Q are polynomial function in x and Q is not the zero polynomial. The domain of f is the set of all points x for which the denominator Q(x) is not zero.

a. Legendre rational functions
b. -equivalence
c. -module
d. Rational function

Chapter 6. Exponential and Logarithmic Functions

1. In mathematics, a commutative ring R is _____ if for any pair of prime ideals

    p, q,

any two strictly increasing chains

   $p=p_0 \subset p_1 ... \subset p_n = q$ of prime ideals

are contained in maximal strictly increasing chains from p to q of the same (finite) length. In other words, there is a well-defined function from pairs of prime ideals to natural numbers, attaching to p and q the length of any such maximal chain.

   a. Chow ring
   b. Quantum cohomology
   c. Catenary
   d. Pencil

2. The _____ of an angle is the ratio of the length of the adjacent side to the length of the hypotenuse. In our case

$$\cos A = \frac{\text{adjacent}}{\text{hypotenuse}} = \frac{b}{h}.$$

The tangent of an angle is the ratio of the length of the opposite side to the length of the adjacent side. In our case

$$\tan A = \frac{\text{opposite}}{\text{adjacent}} = \frac{a}{b}.$$

The remaining three functions are best defined using the above three functions.

   a. -module
   b. -equivalence
   c. 2-bridge knot
   d. Cosine

3. In mathematics, an _____ is the finite or bounded case of a conic section, the geometric shape that results from cutting a circular conical or cylindrical surface with an oblique plane . It is also the locus of all points of the plane whose distances to two fixed points add to the same constant.

Ellipses also arise as images of a circle or a sphere under parallel projection, and some cases of perspective projection.

a. ADE classification
b. AKS primality test
c. Abelian P-root group
d. Ellipse

4. In mathematics, the word _____ is a term for any well-formed combination of mathematical symbols. For example,

$$x^2 + 3x - 4$$

is an _____, while

$$)x) / 0$$

is not, because the parentheses are not balanced and division by zero is undefined.

Being an _____ is a syntactic concept - the meaning of the variables is irrelevant, but different fields have different notions of validity.â€See formal language for how expressions are constructed, and formal semantics for meaning.

a. Orthogonal
b. Unit ring
c. Arity
d. Expression

5. The _____ are natural numbers including 0 ' href='/wiki/0_(number)'>0, 1, 2, 3, ...) and their negatives (0, −1, −2, −3, ...). They are numbers that can be written without a fractional or decimal component, and fall within the set {...
a. Abelian P-root group
b. AKS primality test
c. ADE classification
d. Integers

Chapter 7. Systems of Equations and Inequalities

1. In mathematics, the _____ of a real number is its numerical value without regard to its sign. So, for example, 3 is the _____ of both 3 and −3.

The _____ of a number a is denoted by $|a|$.

   a. AKS primality test
   b. ADE classification
   c. Abelian P-root group
   d. Absolute value

2. In mathematics, an _____ is the finite or bounded case of a conic section, the geometric shape that results from cutting a circular conical or cylindrical surface with an oblique plane . It is also the locus of all points of the plane whose distances to two fixed points add to the same constant.

Ellipses also arise as images of a circle or a sphere under parallel projection, and some cases of perspective projection.

   a. AKS primality test
   b. ADE classification
   c. Ellipse
   d. Abelian P-root group

3. In mathematics, a _____ is a collection of linear equations involving the same set of variables. For example,

$$3x + 2y - z = 1$$
$$2x - 2y + 4z = -2$$
$$-x + \tfrac{1}{2}y - z = 0$$

is a system of three equations in the three variables x, y, z. A solution to a linear system is an assignment of numbers to the variables such that all the equations are simultaneously satisfied.

   a. Simultaneous equations
   b. -equivalence
   c. -module
   d. System of linear equations

4. A _____ is a symbol that stands for a value that may vary; the term usually occurs in opposition to constant, which is a symbol for a non-varying value, i.e. completely fixed or fixed in the context of use. The concepts of constants and variables are fundamental to all modern mathematics, science, engineering, and computer programming.

Chapter 7. Systems of Equations and Inequalities

Much of the basic theory for which we use variables today, such as school geometry and algebra, was developed thousands of years ago, but the use of symbolic formulae and variables is only several hundreds of years old.

a. -module
b. 2-bridge knot
c. -equivalence
d. Variable

5. In linear algebra, _____ is an efficient algorithm for solving systems of linear equations, finding the rank of a matrix, and calculating the inverse of an invertible square matrix. _____ is named after German mathematician and scientist Carl Friedrich Gauss.

Elementary row operations are used to reduce a matrix to row echelon form.

a. 2-bridge knot
b. -equivalence
c. -module
d. Gaussian elimination

6. In mathematics, an _____ is a statement about the relative size or order of two objects, or about whether they are the same or not

- The notation $a < b$ means that a is less than b.
- The notation $a > b$ means that a is greater than b.
- The notation $a \neq b$ means that a is not equal to b, but does not say that one is bigger than the other or even that they can be compared in size.

In all these cases, a is not equal to b, hence, '_____'.

These relations are known as strict _____

- The notation $a \leq b$ means that a is less than or equal to b (or, equivalently, not greater than b);
- The notation $a \geq b$ means that a is greater than or equal to b (or, equivalently, not smaller than b);

An additional use of the notation is to show that one quantity is much greater than another, normally by several orders of magnitude.

- The notation $a \ll b$ means that a is much less than b.
- The notation $a \gg b$ means that a is much greater than b.

Chapter 7. Systems of Equations and Inequalities

If the sense of the _____ is the same for all values of the variables for which its members are defined, then the _____ is called an 'absolute' or 'unconditional' _____. If the sense of an _____ holds only for certain values of the variables involved, but is reversed or destroyed for other values of the variables, it is called a conditional _____.

One can apply the same algebraic operations to inequalities as one would apply for solving equalities. For example, to find x for the _____ 10x > 20 one would divide 20 by 10 to obtain x > 2.

- a. Abelian P-root group
- b. ADE classification
- c. AKS primality test
- d. Inequality

7. In mathematics, the adjective _____ means that an object cannot be expressed as a product of more than one non-trivial factors in a given set. See also factorization.

For any field F, the ring of polynomials with coefficients in F is denoted by F[x].

- a. Alternating polynomial
- b. Ehrhart polynomial
- c. Irreducible
- d. Integer-valued polynomial

8. In mathematics, _____ is a technique for optimization of a linear objective function, subject to linear equality and linear inequality constraints. Informally, _____ determines the way to achieve the best outcome (such as maximum profit or lowest cost) in a given mathematical model and given some list of requirements represented as linear equations.

More formally, given a polytope (for example, a polygon or a polyhedron), and a real-valued affine function

$$f(x_1, x_2, \ldots, x_n) = c_1 x_1 + c_2 x_2 + \cdots + c_n x_n + d$$

defined on this polytope, a _____ method will find a point in the polytope where this function has the smallest (or largest) value.

- a. -equivalence
- b. -module
- c. 2-bridge knot
- d. Linear programming

Chapter 8. Matrices and Determinants

1. In mathematics, a _____ is a rectangular array of numbers. This way, matrices can record data that depend on multiple parameters. In particular they are used to keep track of the coefficients of multiple linear equations. Matrices are closely connected to linear transformations, which are higher-dimensional analogs of linear functions, i.e., functions of the form f(x) = c Â· x, where c is a constant. This map corresponds to a _____ with one row and column, with entry c. In addition to a number of elementary, entrywise operations such as _____ addition a key notion is _____ multiplication, which displays a number of features not encountered in numbers; for example, products of matrices depend on the order of the factors, unlike products of real numbers, say, where c Â· d = d Â· c for any two numbers c and d.

    a. Heap
    b. Commutativity
    c. Polynomial expression
    d. Matrix

2. In mathematics, the _____ of a vector space V is the cardinality (i.e. the number of vectors) of a basis of V. It is sometimes called Hamel _____ or algebraic _____ to distinguish it from other types of _____. All bases of a vector space have equal cardinality and so the _____ of a vector space is uniquely defined. The _____ of the vector space V over the field F can be written as $\dim_F(V)$ or as [V : F], read '_____ of V over F'.

    a. Partial trace
    b. Cofactor
    c. Dual basis
    d. Dimension

3. In mathematics, a _____ is a collection of linear equations involving the same set of variables. For example,

$$3x + 2y - z = 1$$
$$2x - 2y + 4z = -2$$
$$-x + \tfrac{1}{2}y - z = 0$$

is a system of three equations in the three variables x, y, z. A solution to a linear system is an assignment of numbers to the variables such that all the equations are simultaneously satisfied.

    a. System of linear equations
    b. -equivalence
    c. -module
    d. Simultaneous equations

4. In its simplest meaning in mathematics and logic, an _____ is an action or procedure which produces a new value from one or more input values. There are two common types of operations: unary and binary. Unary operations involve only one value, such as negation and trigonometric functions.

Chapter 8. Matrices and Determinants

a. Operation
b. AKS primality test
c. ADE classification
d. Abelian P-root group

5. In linear algebra, _____ is an efficient algorithm for solving systems of linear equations, finding the rank of a matrix, and calculating the inverse of an invertible square matrix. _____ is named after German mathematician and scientist Carl Friedrich Gauss.

Elementary row operations are used to reduce a matrix to row echelon form.

a. 2-bridge knot
b. Gaussian elimination
c. -equivalence
d. -module

6. In mathematics, the _____ of a real number is its numerical value without regard to its sign. So, for example, 3 is the _____ of both 3 and −3.

The _____ of a number a is denoted by $|a|$.

a. ADE classification
b. Abelian P-root group
c. Absolute value
d. AKS primality test

7. A _____ is a symbol that stands for a value that may vary; the term usually occurs in opposition to constant, which is a symbol for a non-varying value, i.e. completely fixed or fixed in the context of use. The concepts of constants and variables are fundamental to all modern mathematics, science, engineering, and computer programming.

Much of the basic theory for which we use variables today, such as school geometry and algebra, was developed thousands of years ago, but the use of symbolic formulae and variables is only several hundreds of years old.

a. 2-bridge knot
b. -module
c. -equivalence
d. Variable

Chapter 8. Matrices and Determinants

8. In mathematics, the complex numbers are an extension of the real numbers obtained by adjoining an imaginary unit, denoted i, which satisfies:

$$i^2 = -1.$$

Every _____ can be written in the form a + bi, where a and b are real numbers called the real part and the imaginary part of the _____, respectively.

Complex numbers are a field, and thus have addition, subtraction, multiplication, and division operations. These operations extend the corresponding operations on real numbers, although with a number of additional elegant and useful properties, e.g., negative real numbers can be obtained by squaring complex (imaginary) numbers.

   a. -module
   b. -equivalence
   c. 2-bridge knot
   d. Complex number

9. _____ is the mathematical process of putting things together. The plus sign '+' means that numbers are added together. For example, in the picture on the right, there are 3 + 2 apples--meaning three apples and two other apples--which is the same as five apples, since 3 + 2 = 5.
   a. AKS primality test
   b. Addition
   c. Abelian P-root group
   d. ADE classification

10. In mathematics, _____ is the operation of adding two matrices by adding the corresponding entries together. However, there is another operation which could also be considered as a kind of addition for matrices.

The usual _____ is defined for two matrices of the same dimensions.

   a. Cofactor
   b. Nonlinear eigenproblem
   c. Projection-valued measure
   d. Matrix addition

11. The real component of a quaternion is also called its _____ part.

Chapter 8. Matrices and Determinants

The term is also sometimes used informally to mean a vector, matrix, tensor, or other usually 'compound' value that is actually reduced to a single component. Thus, for example, the product of a 1×n matrix and an n×1 matrix, which is formally a 1×1 matrix, is often said to be a _____.

   a. Tensor product
   b. Distributivity
   c. Scalar
   d. Self-adjoint

12. A _____ is a three-dimensional solid object bounded by six square faces, facets or sides, with three meeting at each vertex. The _____ can also be called a regular hexahedron and is one of the five Platonic solids. It is a special kind of square prism, of rectangular parallelepiped and of trigonal trapezohedron.
   a. -module
   b. 2-bridge knot
   c. -equivalence
   d. Cube

13. _____ is one of the four basic arithmetic operations; it is the inverse of addition, meaning that if we start with any number and add any number and then subtract the same number we added, we return to the number we started with. _____ is denoted by a minus sign in infix notation.

The traditional names for the parts of the formula

   c − b = a

are minuend (c) − subtrahend (b) = difference (a.)

   a. 2-bridge knot
   b. Subtraction
   c. -module
   d. -equivalence

14. In mathematics, a _____, probability matrix, or transition matrix is used to describe the transitions of a Markov chain. It has found use in probability theory, statistics and linear algebra, as well as computer science. There are several different definitions and types of stochastic matrices;

   A right _____ is a square matrix each of whose rows consists of nonnegative real numbers, with each row summing to 1.

Chapter 8. Matrices and Determinants

a. Bisymmetric matrix
b. Supermatrix
c. Permutation matrix
d. Stochastic Matrix

15. In mathematics, a _____ of a number x is a number r such that r^2 = x, or, in other words, a number r whose square (the result of multiplying the number by itself) is x.

Every non-negative real number x has a unique non-negative _____, called the principal _____, which is denoted with a radical symbol as $\sqrt{x}$, or, using exponent notation, as $x^{1/2}$. For example, the principal _____ of 9 is 3, denoted $\sqrt{9} = 3$, because 3^2 = 3 × 3 = 9.

   a. Square root
   b. 2-bridge knot
   c. -module
   d. -equivalence

16. In mathematics, a _____ of a number x is any number which, when repeatedly multiplied by itself, eventually yields x:

$$r \times r \times \cdots \times r = x.$$

In terms of exponentiation, r is a _____ of x if

$$r^n = x$$

for some positive integer n. For example, 2 is a _____ of 16 since 2^4 = 2 × 2 × 2 × 2 = 16.

The number n is called the degree of the _____.

   a. Cubic function
   b. Root
   c. Rationalisation
   d. Difference of two squares

17. In linear algebra, the _____ or unit matrix of size n is the n-by-n square matrix with ones on the main diagonal and zeros elsewhere. It is denoted by I_n, or simply by I if the size is immaterial or can be trivially determined by the context. (In some fields, such as quantum mechanics, the _____ is denoted by a boldface one, 1; otherwise it is identical to I.)

Chapter 8. Matrices and Determinants

a. Orthogonal
b. Associativity
c. Identity matrix
d. Artinian ideal

18. In linear algebra, the _____ of a matrix A is the collection of cells $A_{i,j}$ where i is equal to j.

The _____ of a square matrix is the diagonal which runs from the top left corner to the bottom right corner. For example, the following matrix has 1s down its _____:

$$\begin{bmatrix} 1 & 0 & 0 \\ 0 & 1 & 0 \\ 0 & 0 & 1 \end{bmatrix}.$$

A square matrix like the above in which the entries outside the _____ are all zero is called a diagonal matrix.

a. Diagonalizable matrix
b. Complex Hadamard matrix
c. Main diagonal
d. Polynomial matrix

19. In algebra, a _____ is a function depending on n that associates a scalar, det(A), to an n×n square matrix A. The fundamental geometric meaning of a _____ is a scale factor for measure when A is regarded as a linear transformation. Determinants are important both in calculus, where they enter the substitution rule for several variables, and in multilinear algebra.

For a fixed nonnegative integer n, there is a unique _____ function for the n×n matrices over any commutative ring R. In particular, this function exists when R is the field of real or complex numbers.

a. Leibniz formula
b. Pfaffian
c. Functional determinant
d. Determinant

20. In mathematics, a _____ is a constant multiplicative factor of a certain object. For example, in the expression $9x^2$, the _____ of x^2 is 9.

The object can be such things as a variable, a vector, a function, etc.

a. Vandermonde polynomial
b. Coefficient
c. Tschirnhaus transformation
d. Constant term

21. In linear algebra, the _____ refers to a matrix consisting of the coefficients of the variables in a set of linear equations.

In general, a system with m linear equations and n unknowns can be written as

$$a_{11}x_1 + a_{12}x_2 + ... + a_{1n}x_n = b_1$$
$$a_{21}x_1 + a_{22}x_2 + ... + a_{2n}x_n = b_2$$
$$\vdots$$
$$a_{m1}x_1 + a_{m2}x_2 + ... + a_{mn}x_n = b_m$$

where $x_1, x_2, ..., x_n$ are the unknowns and the numbers $a_{11}, a_{12}, ..., a_{mn}$ are the coefficients of the system. The _____ is the mxn matrix with the coefficient a_{ij} as the (i,j)-th entry:

$$\begin{bmatrix} a_{11} & a_{12} & \cdots & a_{1n} \\ a_{21} & a_{22} & \cdots & a_{2n} \\ \vdots & \vdots & \ddots & \vdots \\ a_{m1} & a_{m2} & \cdots & a_{mn} \end{bmatrix}$$

a. Centrosymmetric matrix
b. Linear inequality
c. Coefficient matrix
d. Segre classification

22. In mathematics, particularly linear algebra, a _____ is a matrix with all its entries being zero. Some examples of zero matrices are

$$0_{1,1} = \begin{bmatrix} 0 \end{bmatrix}, \ 0_{2,2} = \begin{bmatrix} 0 & 0 \\ 0 & 0 \end{bmatrix}, \ 0_{2,3} = \begin{bmatrix} 0 & 0 & 0 \\ 0 & 0 & 0 \end{bmatrix},$$

The set of m×n matrices with entries in a ring K forms a ring $K_{m,n}$. The _____ $0_{K_{m,n}}$ in $K_{m,n}$ is the matrix with all entries equal to 0_K, where 0_K is the additive identity in K.

a. Zero matrix
b. Complex Hadamard matrix
c. Regular Hadamard matrix
d. Normal matrix

23. In linear algebra, a _____ of a matrix A is the determinant of some smaller square matrix, cut down from A by removing one or more of its rows or columns. Minors obtained by removing just one row and one column from square matrices (first minors) are required for calculating matrix cofactors, which in turn are useful for computing both the determinant and inverse of square matrices.
   a. Rng
   b. Supergroup
   c. Purification
   d. Minor

24. In mathematics, an _____ is the finite or bounded case of a conic section, the geometric shape that results from cutting a circular conical or cylindrical surface with an oblique plane . It is also the locus of all points of the plane whose distances to two fixed points add to the same constant.

Ellipses also arise as images of a circle or a sphere under parallel projection, and some cases of perspective projection.

   a. Abelian P-root group
   b. AKS primality test
   c. ADE classification
   d. Ellipse

25. A _____ is one of the basic shapes of geometry: a polygon with three corners or vertices and three sides or edges which are line segments. A _____ with vertices A, B, and C is denoted ABC.

In Euclidean geometry any three non-collinear points determine a unique _____ and a unique plane (i.e. a two-dimensional Euclidean space.)

   a. -module
   b. -equivalence
   c. Triangle
   d. 2-bridge knot

26. In mathematics, a _____ is a flat surface. Planes can arise as subspaces of some higher dimensional space, as with the walls of a room, or they may enjoy an independent existence in their own right, as in the setting of Euclidean geometry
   a. Plane
   b. -module
   c. Similarity
   d. -equivalence

Chapter 9. Conic Sections   53

1. In mathematics, a _____ is a curve obtained by intersecting a cone (more precisely, a circular conical surface) with a plane. A _____ is therefore a restriction of a quadric surface to the plane. The conic sections were named and studied as long ago as 200 BC, when Apollonius of Perga undertook a systematic study of their properties.
   a. Dandelin spheres
   b. Conic section
   c. Matrix representation of conic sections
   d. Derivation of the cartesian form for an ellipse

2. In mathematics, an _____ is the finite or bounded case of a conic section, the geometric shape that results from cutting a circular conical or cylindrical surface with an oblique plane . It is also the locus of all points of the plane whose distances to two fixed points add to the same constant.

Ellipses also arise as images of a circle or a sphere under parallel projection, and some cases of perspective projection.

   a. Ellipse
   b. ADE classification
   c. Abelian P-root group
   d. AKS primality test

3. In mathematics, the _____ is a conic section, the intersection of a right circular conical surface and a plane parallel to a generating straight line of that surface. Given a point (the focus) and a line (the directrix) that lie in a plane, the locus of points in that plane that are equidistant to them is a _____.

A particular case arises when the plane is tangent to the conical surface of a circle.

   a. -module
   b. -equivalence
   c. 2-bridge knot
   d. Parabola

4. In the mathematical field of topology, a _____ of a fiber bundle, π: E → B, over a topological space, B, is a continuous map, s : B → E, such that π(s(x))=x for all x in B.

A _____ is a certain generalization of the notion of the graph of a function. The graph of a function g : X → Y can be identified with a function taking its values in the Cartesian product E = X×Y of X and Y:

$$s(x) = (x, g(x)) \in E, \quad s : X \to E.$$

A _____ is an abstract characterization of what it means to be a graph.

a. -module
b. Fiber bundle
c. -equivalence
d. Section

5. In geometry, a _____ of a circle is any straight line segment that passes through the center of the circle and whose endpoints are on the circle. The diameters are the longest chords of the circle. The word '_____' derives from Greek δiῆμετρος , 'diagonal of a circle', from δια- (dia-), 'across, through' + μῖτρον (metron), 'a measure'.)

a. Diameter
b. -module
c. -equivalence
d. 2-bridge knot

6. In geometry, the foci, pronounced , are a pair of special points used in describing conic sections. The four types of conic sections are the circle, parabola, ellipse, and hyperbola.

The _____ has two equivalent defining properties; and they always fall on the major axis of symmetry of the conic.

a. Conic section
b. Dandelin spheres
c. Derivation of the cartesian form for an ellipse
d. Focus

7. The term _____ or centre is used in various contexts in abstract algebra to denote the set of all those elements that commute with all other elements. More specifically:

- The _____ of a group G consists of all those elements x in G such that xg = gx for all g in G. This is a normal subgroup of G.
- The _____ of a ring R is the subset of R consisting of all those elements x of R such that xr = rx for all r in R. The _____ is a commutative subring of R, so R is an algebra over its _____.
- The _____ of an algebra A consists of all those elements x of A such that xa = ax for all a in A. See also: central simple algebra.
- The _____ of a Lie algebra L consists of all those elements x in L such that [x,a] = 0 for all a in L. This is an ideal of the Lie algebra L.
- The _____ of a monoidal category C consists of pairs (A,u) where A is an object of C, and $u : A \otimes - \to - \otimes A$ a natural isomorphism satisfying certain axioms.

a. Center
b. Ring theory
c. Self-adjoint
d. Left alternative

8. In abstract algebra, the _____ of a module is a measure of the module's 'size'. It is defined as the _____ of the longest ascending chain of submodules and is a generalization of the concept of dimension for vector spaces. The modules with finite _____ share many important properties with finite-dimensional vector spaces.
   a. Supermodule
   b. Morita equivalence
   c. Finitely generated module
   d. Length

9. In linear algebra, a _____ of a matrix A is the determinant of some smaller square matrix, cut down from A by removing one or more of its rows or columns. Minors obtained by removing just one row and one column from square matrices (first minors) are required for calculating matrix cofactors, which in turn are useful for computing both the determinant and inverse of square matrices.
   a. Minor
   b. Rng
   c. Purification
   d. Supergroup

10. In mathematics, the _____, denoted e or ε, is a parameter associated with every conic section. It can be thought of as a measure of how much the conic section deviates from being circular.

In particular,

- The _____ of a circle is zero.
- The _____ of an (non-circle) ellipse is greater than zero but less than 1.
- The _____ of a parabola is 1.
- The _____ of a hyperbola is greater than 1.

Furthermore, two conic sections are similar if and only if they have the same _____.

For every conic section, there exists a fixed focus point F, a fixed line L and a non-negative number e such that the conic section consists of all points whose distance to F equals e times their distance to L, a directrix.

a. AKS primality test
b. Eccentricity
c. Abelian P-root group
d. ADE classification

11. In linear algebra, a _____ is a linear transformation that squares to the identity ($R^2 = I$, where R is in K dimensional space), also known as an involution in the general linear group. In addition to reflections across hyperplanes, the class of general reflections includes point reflections, reflections across subspaces of intermediate dimension, and non-orthogonal reflections.

A _____ over a hyperplane in an inner product space is necessarily symmetric, but a general _____ need not be as the example $\begin{bmatrix} 1 & 0 \\ 1 & -1 \end{bmatrix}$ shows.

a. Homomorphic secret sharing
b. Reflection
c. Morphism
d. Shear mappings

12. In mathematics, a _____ in a topological space X is a continuous map f from the unit interval I = [0,1] to X

$f : I \to X$.

The initial point of the _____ is f(0) and the terminal point is f(1.) One often speaks of a '_____ from x to y' where x and y are the initial and terminal points of the _____.

a. Suspension
b. Genus
c. Path
d. Simplicial complex

13. In geometry, a _____ is a straight curve. When geometry is used to model the real world, lines are used to represent straight objects with negligible width and height. Lines are an idealisation of such objects and have no width or height at all and are usually considered to be infinitely long.
a. -equivalence
b. 2-bridge knot
c. -module
d. Line

Chapter 10. Sequences and Series

1. In algebra, a commutative ring R is said to be _____ if any of the following equivalent conditions holds:

    1. The localization R_m of R at m is a valuation ring for every maximal ideal m of R.
    2. For all ideals $\mathfrak{a}$, $\mathfrak{b}$, and $\mathfrak{c}$,

    $$\mathfrak{a} \cap (\mathfrak{b} + \mathfrak{c}) = (\mathfrak{a} \cap \mathfrak{b}) + (\mathfrak{a} \cap \mathfrak{c})$$

- For all ideals $\mathfrak{a}$, $\mathfrak{b}$, and $\mathfrak{c}$,

$$\mathfrak{a} + (\mathfrak{b} \cap \mathfrak{c}) = (\mathfrak{a} + \mathfrak{b}) \cap (\mathfrak{a} + \mathfrak{c})$$

An _____ domain is called a Prüfer domain.

   a. Exchange matrix
   b. Ordered vector space
   c. Inverse eigenvalues theorem
   d. Arithmetical

2. In mathematics, specifically group theory, the _____ of a subgroup H in a group G is the e;relative sizee; of H in G. For example, if H has _____ 2 in G, then intuitively e;halfe; of the elements of G lie in H. The _____ of H in G is usually denoted |G : H| or [G : H].

If G and H are finite groups, then the _____ of H in G is simply the quotient of the orders of the two groups:

$$|G : H| = \frac{|G|}{|H|}.$$

By Lagrange's theorem, this number is always a positive integer.

If G and H are infinite, then the _____ of H is G is defined as the number of cosets of H in G.

   a. Even permutations
   b. Index
   c. Inner automorphism
   d. Outer automorphism

3. A _____ is a symbol that stands for a value that may vary; the term usually occurs in opposition to constant, which is a symbol for a non-varying value, i.e. completely fixed or fixed in the context of use. The concepts of constants and variables are fundamental to all modern mathematics, science, engineering, and computer programming.

Chapter 10. Sequences and Series

Much of the basic theory for which we use variables today, such as school geometry and algebra, was developed thousands of years ago, but the use of symbolic formulae and variables is only several hundreds of years old.

a. -equivalence
b. -module
c. 2-bridge knot
d. Variable

4. A _____ is an expression which compares quantities relative to each other. The most common examples involve two quantities, but in theory any number of quantities can be compared. In mathematical terms, they are represented by separating each quantity with a colon, for example the _____ 2:3, which is read as the _____ 'two to three'.

a. Rational number
b. Number system
c. -equivalence
d. Ratio

5. In mathematics, a _____ is a series with a constant ratio between successive terms. For example, the series

$$\frac{1}{2} + \frac{1}{4} + \frac{1}{8} + \frac{1}{16} + \cdots$$

is geometric, because each term is equal to half of the previous term. The sum of this series is 1, as illustrated in the following picture:

_____ are one of the simplest examples of infinite series with finite sums.

a. Geometric series
b. -module
c. -equivalence
d. 2-bridge knot

Chapter 10. Sequences and Series

6. In elementary algebra, a _____ is a polynomial with two terms--the sum of two monomials--often bound by parenthesis or brackets when operated upon. It is the simplest kind of polynomial other than monomials.

   - The _____ $a^2 - b^2$ can be factored as the product of two other binomials:

     $a^2 - b^2 = (a + b)(a - b.)$

     This is a special case of the more general formula:

     $$a^{n+1} - b^{n+1} = (a - b) \sum_{k=0}^{n} a^k b^{n-k}.$$

   - The product of a pair of linear binomials $(ax + b)$ and $(cx + d)$ is:

     $(ax + b)(cx + d) = acx^2 + axd + bcx + bd.$

   - A _____ raised to the nth power, represented as

     $(a + b)^n$

     can be expanded by means of the _____ theorem or, equivalently, using Pascal's triangle. Taking a simple example, the perfect square _____ $(p + q)^2$ can be found by squaring the :first digit, adding twice the product of the first and second digit and finally adding the square of the second digit, to give $p^2 + 2pq + q^2$.

   a. Content
   b. Theory of equations
   c. Generalized arithmetic progression
   d. Binomial

7. A _____ is one of the basic shapes of geometry: a polygon with three corners or vertices and three sides or edges which are line segments. A _____ with vertices A, B, and C is denoted ABC.

   In Euclidean geometry any three non-collinear points determine a unique _____ and a unique plane (i.e. a two-dimensional Euclidean space.)

   a. -module
   b. -equivalence
   c. 2-bridge knot
   d. Triangle

8. In mathematics, a _____ is a constant multiplicative factor of a certain object. For example, in the expression $9x^2$, the _____ of x^2 is 9.

The object can be such things as a variable, a vector, a function, etc.

a. Constant term
b. Coefficient
c. Vandermonde polynomial
d. Tschirnhaus transformation

9. In mathematics, the _____ is an important formula giving the expansion of powers of sums. Its simplest version states that

$$(x+y)^n = \sum_{k=0}^{n} \binom{n}{k} x^{n-k} y^k \qquad (1)$$

for any real or complex numbers x and y, and any non-negative integer n. The binomial coefficient appearing in (1) may be defined in terms of the factorial function n!:

$$\binom{n}{k} = \frac{n!}{k!\,(n-k)!}.$$

For example, here are the cases where 2 ≤ n ≤ 5:

$$(x+y)^2 = x^2 + 2xy + y^2$$
$$(x+y)^3 = x^3 + 3x^2y + 3xy^2 + y^3$$
$$(x+y)^4 = x^4 + 4x^3y + 6x^2y^2 + 4xy^3 + y^4$$
$$(x+y)^5 = x^5 + 5x^4y + 10x^3y^2 + 10x^2y^3 + 5xy^4 + y^5.$$

Formula (1) is valid more generally for any elements x and y of a semiring as long as xy = yx.

a. Binomial Theorem
b. -equivalence
c. 2-bridge knot
d. -module

10. In mathematics, an _____ of a product of sums expresses it as a sum of products by using the fact that multiplication distributes over addition. Expansions of polynomials are obtained by multiplying together their factors, which results in a sum of terms with variables raised to different degrees.

To multiply two factors, each term of the first factor must be multiplied by each term of the other factor.

a. Analytic subgroup
b. Ordered vector space
c. Equipotential surfaces
d. Expansion

Chapter 11. Counting and Probability

1. In several fields of mathematics the term _____ is used with different but closely related meanings. They all relate to the notion of mapping the elements of a set to other elements of the same set, i.e., exchanging (or 'permuting') elements of a set.

The general concept of _____ can be defined more formally in different contexts:

In combinatorics, a _____ is usually understood to be a sequence containing each element from a finite set once, and only once.

   a. Near-field
   b. Binary function
   c. Rupture field
   d. Permutation

2. In linear algebra, the _____ describes a particular construction that is useful for calculating both the determinant and inverse of square matrices. Specifically the _____ of the (i, j) entry of a matrix, also known as the (i, j) _____ of that matrix, is the signed minor of that entry.

Finding the minors of a matrix A is a multi-step process:

   1. Choose an entry a_{ij} from the matrix.
   2. Cross out the entries that lie in the corresponding row i and column j.
   3. Rewrite the matrix without the marked entries.
   4. Obtain the determinant M_{ij} of this new matrix.

M_{ij} is termed the minor for entry a_{ij}.

If i + j is an even number, the _____ C_{ij} of a_{ij} coincides with its minor:

$$C_{ij} = M_{ij}.$$

Otherwise, it is equal to the additive inverse of its minor:

$$C_{ij} = -M_{ij}.$$

If A is a square matrix, then the minor of its entry a_{ij}, also known as the i,j, or (i,j), or (i,j)[th] minor of A, is denoted by M_{ij} and is defined to be the determinant of the submatrix obtained by removing from A its i-th row and j-th column.

a. Complex structure
b. Cofactor
c. Coefficient matrix
d. Resolvent set

3. In discrete mathematics and predominantly in set theory, a _____ is a concept used in comparisons of sets to refer to the unique values of one set in relation to another. The terms 'absolute' and 'relative' _____ refer to more specific applications of the concept, with universal complements referring to elements unique to the universal set and the latter referring to the unique elements of one set in relation to another. In this image, the universal set is represented by the border of the image, and the set A as a disc.

   a. Pointed set
   b. -equivalence
   c. -module
   d. Complement

4. In set theory, the term _____ refers to a set operation used in the convergence of set elements to form a resultant set containing the elements of both sets. As a simple example, a _____ of two disjoint sets, which do not have elements in common results in a set containing all elements from both sets. A Venn diagram representing the _____ of sets A and B. If one circle represents A, and the other B, then the red area represents the _____ of A and B. The area where the circles join, also shown in red, is the intersection of the two sets.

   If we define two sets which contain unique elements; those of A not occurring in B and vice versa, then the _____ of these sets results in a set which contains all elements of A and B. In terms of notation, we could define this set operation as the following:

   A = {1,2,3,4}
   B = {5,6,7,8}
   $$A \cup B = \{1, 2, 3, 4, 5, 6, 7, 8\}$$

   Other more complex operations can be done including the _____, if the set is for example defined by a property rather than a finite or assumed infinite enumeration of elements.

   a. AKS primality test
   b. Abelian P-root group
   c. Union
   d. ADE classification

5. In mathematics, the _____ of two sets A and B is the set that contains all elements of A that also belong to B (or equivalently, all elements of B that also belong to A), but no other elements.

Chapter 11. Counting and Probability

For explanation of the symbols used in this article, refer to the table of mathematical symbols.

The _____ of A and B

The _____ of A and B is written 'A ∩ B'.

a. Intersection
b. ADE classification
c. Abelian P-root group
d. AKS primality test

6. In elementary algebra, a _____ is a polynomial with two terms--the sum of two monomials--often bound by parenthesis or brackets when operated upon. It is the simplest kind of polynomial other than monomials.

- The _____ a² - b² can be factored as the product of two other binomials:

    a² - b² = (a + b)(a - b.)

    This is a special case of the more general formula:
    $$a^{n+1} - b^{n+1} = (a - b) \sum_{k=0}^{n} a^k b^{n-k}.$$

- The product of a pair of linear binomials (ax + b) and (cx + d) is:

    (ax + b)(cx + d) = acx² + axd + bcx + bd.

- A _____ raised to the nth power, represented as

    (a + b)^n

    can be expanded by means of the _____ theorem or, equivalently, using Pascal's triangle. Taking a simple example, the perfect square _____ (p + q)² can be found by squaring the :first digit, adding twice the product of the first and second digit and finally adding the square of the second digit, to give p² + 2pq + q².

a. Content
b. Generalized arithmetic progression
c. Theory of equations
d. Binomial

ANSWER KEY

Chapter 1
1. b   2. c   3. d   4. d   5. d   6. c   7. a   8. b   9. d   10. c
11. b   12. b   13. b   14. d   15. d   16. d   17. d   18. d   19. c   20. c
21. a   22. a   23. b   24. c   25. b   26. d   27. d   28. d

Chapter 2
1. d   2. d   3. d   4. a   5. d   6. d   7. b   8. d   9. d   10. c
11. b   12. d   13. c   14. b   15. a   16. d   17. d   18. a   19. b   20. a
21. a   22. d

Chapter 3
1. d   2. a   3. d   4. d   5. b   6. d   7. a   8. a   9. d   10. b
11. b

Chapter 4
1. a   2. a   3. b   4. d   5. a   6. b   7. d   8. b   9. d   10. b
11. d   12. d   13. b   14. b   15. d   16. c   17. d   18. d   19. b

Chapter 5
1. a   2. b   3. a   4. d   5. b   6. a   7. d   8. d   9. a   10. d
11. d   12. a   13. d   14. d   15. d

Chapter 6
1. c   2. d   3. d   4. d   5. d

Chapter 7
1. d   2. c   3. d   4. d   5. d   6. d   7. c   8. d

Chapter 8
1. d   2. d   3. a   4. a   5. b   6. c   7. d   8. d   9. b   10. d
11. c   12. d   13. b   14. d   15. a   16. b   17. c   18. c   19. d   20. b
21. c   22. a   23. d   24. d   25. c   26. a

Chapter 9
1. b   2. a   3. d   4. d   5. a   6. d   7. a   8. d   9. a   10. b
11. b   12. c   13. d

Chapter 10
1. d   2. b   3. d   4. d   5. a   6. d   7. d   8. b   9. a   10. d

Chapter 11
1. d   2. b   3. d   4. c   5. a   6. d